RACISM
RACISM
RACISM

RACISM
RACISM
RACISM

BEHIND THE SCHOOLHOUSE
WALLS

Senamu Stelae

Copyright © 2003 by Senamu Stelae
ISBN: 1-4134-3837-7

All rights reserved. No part of this book may be reproduced or transmitted in any form or by any means, electronic or mechanical, including photocopying, recording, or by any information storage and retrieval system, without permission in writing from the author.

Events may be real but names have been fictionalized to protect the innocent.

This book was printed in the United States of America.

Prologue

"In 1661 laws were passed to protect the investments of whites by placing Blacks in a state of perpetual servitude" (Webster 1974)

2003 – RACISM STILL EXISTS! It is more covert and engrained in mainline reasoning.

Even our educational system still fosters this mentality. I will lead you on a path through my eyes and the experiences of other Black people as their stories were relayed to me.

Slavery was outlawed in 1865 and it has been an upward struggle for Black people ever since. We were given the right to vote in 1965 and all through society there has been so-called constant change. Has racism changed with it or has it gone underground in our systems of values. Who are the authors of the textbooks that are used in our classrooms? Who really approve their usage? Who really decides how it is presented? Who really lay the groundwork for what is considered acceptable or not? Who is the hierarchy within the hierarchy? Who is whispering in Caesar's ear?

Summary

These facts are self-evident and you can take them for what their worth. With an open-eye and mind you can see that things really haven't changed. To the reader, form your own opinion based on the facts that you read in this book.

Is institutionalized racism a part of an overarching goal to preserve white supremacy? Are public schools being used as a launching pad to foster subjugation or is it solely for the purpose of preserving the position of the decreasing white population? You decide.

Senamu Stelae

Special thanks go out to Anthony Bentley, a friend, a confident, and the left side of my brain.

Also, I would like to thank all of my contributors for without their perspective this book would not be possible.

Contents

Prologue 5

Summary 7

Case Study #1 15

Case Study #2 31

Case Study #3 39
    Satan's Principal 39
    Observation Day 46

Case Study #4 51

Racism, Racism, Racism, Behind the Schoolhouse Walls

Case Study #1

The walls are permeated with the voices of white teachers echoing their hostilities and resentments of, "Who does she think she is?" referring to something that black teacher has said. It's always misinterpreted. Racism, Racism, Racism. There are those *white* teachers with some authority. It gives them authority over white teachers. It gives them *supremacy* over black teachers. 'They abuse their power. They enjoy this abuse. She yells, "Tote that barge, lift that bail!" And do it Now! Don't talk back, don't utter a word or they'll get you. The others. They will infiltrate the culture of power with their "looks", their "evil eyes" their "hateful words". One parent shouts, I don't want my child honoring Dr. King. Who does that nigger think she is?! The words are repeated by yet another parent in the background. Some of them are afraid to be seen. Their hatred is subtle but noticeable. "He'll get a gift but I'm not going to give "her" one! The child repeats this. *Confusion!*

Racism, Racism, Racism, Administration turns away. What to do? What to do? A clouded picture of what's going on. He allows it to go on. It's so far out of control. There is no turning back. Not now. Massah is against you. You feel powerless but in your powerful position you had a chance and you let it slip away. Now the walls are crumbling all around you. You abandoned me! You left me alone with them! Oh, I forgot, you're one of them too, aren't you? They can hold their own without you anyway. You were always just a silent voice (too many voiceovers) they'll enjoy the show won't they? After all, when the actors and actresses are finished everyone one applauds. Lots of laughter and content. That's the way they like it. Oh, by the way, hold the door nigger. Practice back stage but keep your mouth shut. Sh-h-h-h—don't make a noise until we tell you to. NOW! ACTION! DANCE NIGGER DANCE! You ran away! You turned your back! Dehumanized! Desensitized! Now it's too late!

"Don't you ever do that again!" He points his finger in the black man's face. "You're nothing, you're not important. Your feelings do not matter. Do what I say now or I'll make your life outside of here a living hell as well!" The black man takes it in deeper and deeper. It's too painful. Too hard to swallow. Take it, you have to or else! Oh, No! Look what I have done! I'm less than a man! I don't deserve to be respected. *I apologize.* Walk away and take your sorrows with you. Walk away, black man or else? Racism. Racism, Racism. He says, "We're still slaves aren't we?" 'Yes".

Valentine's Day's hearts are displayed on classroom doors. THIS IS BLACK HISTORY MONTH! "I'll have my children read a poem she says as the "other teachers" clamor and clatter "the room, making coffee, marking worksheets, gossiping, and marking their calenders for the next school field trip or "free-day while getting paid day." THIS IS BLACK HISTORY MONTH! CAN ANYONE HEAR ME! No! "Her again!" "Who else has a child to talk about?

THIS IS BLACK HISTORY MONTH CAN ANYONE HEAR ME? No! Meeting Adjourned. You put on a big production. He came into your room 3 xs but who knows, maybe just maybe. Off, on. Off, on. Well, I don't know if you'll be able to do it. On today, off today. A whole week of this, too stressful. I won't do it again next year. Whew, what a relief! Too Long. Too much. Too good. We don't want to think about it that long. TURN IT OFF!

Racism, Racism, Racism. She didn't do it the

next year. King! King! King! Some of us do recognize him. He's acceptable to most of us, but only one of them or maybe two but no more than three. I guess we should be grateful for that much. We are MASSAH! We sure are! But what about, Malcolm, Hannibal, Evans, Hughes, Turner, Akhatenon, Prossier, Turner, Vessey, and all the others? Why not you? Oh, I forgot. You're not acceptable! You're not comfortable thoughts! You're not humans!

Racism, Racism, Racism, behind the schoolhouse walls. Berates me in front of the children. Berates me in front of the teachers. Berates me in front of the parents. In the Yard! Hallways! Auditorium! BERATES! BERATES! BERATES! Don't talk to me like that! Stop calling me by my first name! Okay, she replies, and she calls me by my first name once again. They talk about it in the hallways, as your walking by. They get silent and then, as you get further down the hallway, they snicker, and make quiet remarks but you hear them. You are fine tuned but they don't know it.

Racism, Racism, Racism reversed. Run to your white Massah. Be my servant! Obey my wishes! Do what I say, now, don't disobey me! I'll get you! Don't think! Just slide across yeah! Just slide across! Yeah! Do that dance! Make me laugh! Don't think! Don't verbalize! Just slide across! Yeah! Smack those big lips! Shut your mouth! Don't you think you know more than me! Bob your head! Shake those big hips! Just slide and shuffle, slide and shuffle. Yeah! That's right pretty nigger!

"What can I do?" he says to me. I don't know what to do. I have to deal with this everyday. I don't know what to do. I'm tired of him treating me like a dog. That's what they *use* to think of us. They *still* do. I don't know what to do.

"GET YOUR OWN!" I said. YOU GOT SKILLS BOY!

They sent their kids in out of the cold. Mine was still out there. "Go, get your kids! She screams at the top of her lungs in the quiet hallway. She wasn't even a teacher. But she felt powerful. "You're late anyway, so hurry up!" shouts a white woman in front of the parents and children. They stood and watched and waited. You didn't react, at least not in the way they wanted and expected you to. Not the way you're perceived, not the way the "others' make you appear to be. You took the abuse in stride. Use your shield of intelligence girl! Yeah, that will work! That will get them every time. "Thank-you", I said. Are we ready children? As you walk away with your well managed class, you can hear the evil sneers. "Who does she think she is? Pass down the hallway and see the frozen smile, the stale faces, and the ugly sneers. DON'T SPEAK! YOU DON'T HAVE TO SPEAK TO ME! I'M NOT HUMAN YOU KNOW! I'M NOT ONE OF YOU! I'M DIFFERENT! I KNOW. I DON'T ACT LIKE YOU AND I DON'T WANT TO. I DON'T KNOW WHY. WHO DO I THINK I AM? We know that! The same group has now moved to the office. You get a phone call from the office. You don't have trip slips they said. Then she, lady supremacy comes breaking your door down. Shouting across the room, you don't have trip slips you can't go you'll have to stay here! Why didn't you have trip slips? She calls me by my first name again. Next time have trip slips signed!! You'll have to let the lunchroom know! Okay, Massah of supremacy, I'll— and she slams the door in the middle of my sentence.

As you walk pass the lobby to go on your break the group has now dispersed but one lingers on and says, "Sorry". You force a fake smile and walk quietly away. She joins with a different crowd that is a mainstay of the school lobby. The overseers, both black and white. "Who does she think she is? While on break, its freedom time! Get away! Get as far away as you can from them. Oh, but their all around you, but they don't know who I am. This is different. You can take those evil glances and ignorant jesters and walk away. You can choose whether or not to see them tomorrow. It's different and it feels good. Well, time to read the paper. BLACK MAN DIES AFTER FATAL SHOOOTING. THE DEATH RATE OF

BLACKS IS HIGHER THAN WHITES. BLACK INMATES REBEL AGAINST WHITE GUARDS – 3 DIE. A BLACK MAN RUNS FOR THE PRESIDENCY – IS THIS A JOKE SAYS ONE TALK SHOW HOST. BLACK WOMEN DIE OF BREAST CANCER AT RATES MUCH HIGHER THAN WHITE WOMEN. BLACKS LIFE EXPECTANCY IS MUCH LOWER THAN WHITES. PAGE AFTER PAGE AFTER PAGE! SCHOOL CLOSINGS IN PREDOMINATELY BLACK NEIGHBORHOODS. PAGE AFTER PAGE AFTER PAGE PAGE. OBITUARIES – NAME AFTER NAME AFTER NAME. Flip through the radio stations. "Who do they think they are! We don't owe then anything! They make me sick! I don't want them in my neighborhood. My property value has gone down! Why did they tear the projects down! Let them keep on shooting one another. I don't care!

Build more prisons! We've given them enough! I flip to *that* radio station. *You know, the one about my people. The one that makes me feel proud.* I feel g-oo-d. Thank-you! Congratulations Black man! You've got your own. But be careful. Be cautious. They're watching you. Don't make a mistake. Cross your T's and dot your I's or they'll get you.

That will be $25.96 . She looks for the magic brown pen to slide across the $5 and $10 dollar bills. I thought it was for only $20 and up. Don't ask Don't say nothing,. Just take it and get out. I don't trust you! Take a deep breath 1 . . . 2 . . . 3 . . . 4 . . . 5 . . . 6 . . . 7 . . . 8 . . . 9 . . . . 10.

It's time to go back now. You can do it! You know you can girl! You've done it all these years. You've endured the pain, anguish, rejection, isolation, beratement, degradation, hostility, hatred, insults, sneers, jeers, interruptions, ignorance, intolerance, dissociation, humiliation, intimidation, and frustration. As you forced the doors open, you feel the suction. Something is pulling you back but you muster the strength that you will need to get you through. There they are. They greet you at the door. "She's so quiet". You walk away gracefully like a stallion- quickly though, get through the other doors. Don't make a sound. Don't utter a word. You'll be safe soon. Close your door and you won't hear them. But the walls are very thin. They built them that way.

She screams as you pick up your class. He did this and he did that and he has a detention. You say as soft spoken as you can amongst the loud voices of busy children. Could you write it down so the parent will know all of the details? She looks at you in amazement and abruptly exits the auditorium. Later on she reluctantly hands you the detention slip. Could you please write down the reason so the parent will know? Later on she gives it to you in a huff, this time she has an audience.

You pass by just enough to hear them say. WHO DOES SHE THINK SHE IS! A white woman said you have a lot of discipline problems. Why do I have more than you? I don't know, your black, you can handle it. We want it that way. This is the way it is and it ain't nothun you can do about it! SMILE NIGGER SMILE! He took one of your best students out of your classroom and put her in another black teacher's classroom. Divide and conquer. Ain't it grand! Tried and True! Tried and True! You asked why and he said because she didn't talk much. He never asked for your opinion but your opinion doesn't matter even if you were asked. Don't you know that girl!

Over the holidays. "I got so many presents, I have to take some of them to the car and come back for the rest!" She said gleefully. Oh I forgot, let me go back and get the one present that I got. I can't wait to open it. COOKIE DOUGH. Just what I wanted. The white child is happy to have made the gesture. She doesn't know the whole ugly story. She'll see the full picture as she gets older. Some of them know it now. Her parents will make sure of it. "Thanks sweetie". The black kids made me cards and some of the others did too. I got lots of hand made cards and one that was purchased. I hung them up on the windows, door, and heating pipes for all to see. Look at me, they love me unconditionally. I am the person, you know, "Who does she think she is? How can you smile in spite of it all? Don't you know what we're doing to you? Don't you know what we can do to you? Don't be happy! Unless we want you to. Otherwise Don't feel. After all your not human. **YOU GOT THROUGH ANOTHER DAY. YOU GO GIRL!**

Case Study #2

Albert Ralph, I spotted you on 95N walking with your cane. I pulled over and hesitated, I wasn't sure how you would react. You weren't sure about me either. But I stopped. They told me to fear you. They told you to fear me but they can't control this part of me. I keep it hidden. I walked toward you and you me. I saw your eyes from a distance. You saw me. I knew it was alright. They didn't get to you yet or did they? Your face, so sad, so many stories to tell. Where are you going? Across the highway about ¼ of a mile. On the south side there was a tow truck. I'm going to ask him to tow me. If you go across this highway you'll get killed!

He looked so sad. Do you have AAA (Triple AAA)? I don't know. He pulls out a saturated with age leather black wallet. My hands are bad. I can't . . . But he managed to take out the card. Eureka! AAA card. I pulled out my cell phone and dialed the 800 number. I need help for Albert Ralph. The number is . . . . .You must be the best thing that ever happened to me . . . . I smiled. A police officer pulled up. Albert Ralph seemed real happy to see him. I know, Albert, you were taught that way. Ain't conditioning good. I hesitated and waited. Nothing happened. The tow truck will be here in 60 minutes or less. What did you say your name was again? Albert Ralph. Are you hungry? Are you a diabetic? Are you thirsty? No, Albert said. I'm alright. The police officer is here with me. No, Albert he's not going to stay with you. No, I have to go, he interrupted. Do you want to wait in my car? No, I can call someone for you. He laughs, I'm okay. Then the officer said, "There is no one that would have done what you did." Thank-you. Albert, I won't forget you. I won't forget you either. I have a story to tell you too. No, I think you already know, I said silently.

The next day I received a memo that read, please come to my office at your earliest convenience." He has only 90 days before he retires in June. So, he works only once or twice a week. Anyhow, I know what it is in reference to. A white teacher came to my room the other day and attempted to hand me some flyers for a field trip to the movies to see a cartoon about Neemo. I said, "I'm not going". She looked in astonishment. "Excuse me?" she said with indignation. I'm not going. Why? I thought it was on a volunteer basis. So I'm not going. Isn't this pertaining to a cartoon about Neemo? She replied, "Yes!" I'm assuming that she went to massuh and now he wants to see me in his office. The other white woman who promenades up and down the hallways like a trashy queen can say anything and do anything that she wants to do at anytime and no one will question or even give her a dirty look much more go and tell massuh. One day she yelled, "I'm not taking my class out to recess. It's too cold. Why did she (referring to the black (house servant VP) say that its outdoor recess, she must be crazy. I'm not going on that field trip. I'll stay here and watch the kids that are not going. I'm not this and I'm not that!

He didn't pay attention to me when I asked for a meeting to discuss the controversy with the ESOl teacher. It wasn't that important, I guess. But this time it is. It's important that I go to see the cartoon about Neemo.

Today, he told the other first grade teacher to go into my room to search for the "blue and yellow" cards. She of course followed orders and rummaged through my desk drawers looking for these cards that he had to have IMMEDIATELY! After conversing with her about it, she said, I really didn't want to do it but he said, "I need it now!" He did not have the courtesy to let us know or let me know ahead of time by making an announcement or sending a memo. She said, "I waited an hour for the other teacher's cards." Oh, she added. "I went through the cards and changed some of the "D's" in behavior and moved them to another class so it can be equitable. I'm just trying to be fair. FAIR! FAIR! FAIR! When has anyone ever been fair? It's all about getting what you want or helping your girlfriends and if you're not in with the crowd, you are going to get the rough end of the stick. I'm used to it. I'm used to it. I'm just tired of it.

This is the norm for most schools. The "group" dissects classes "at will". If "they" don't like you, you will not only be ostracized but condemned to hell with a classroom full of students that they deem as "rejects" "misfits" "too slow" "low reading levels" "borderline special education" "mentally ill (unclinically diagnosed) "on medication" "pre-special education-but no room at the end" "disruptive" "retarded (in their minds" "incorrigible" "problematic" "parents-get-on-your – fuckin nerves and I don't want that child in my class" "sickening child" – and the list goes on and on and on. You'll be stuck with these kids. But, if you're good and you know you're good then it will be"piece of cake" bitchy parents and all. You'll get through. You have to. You have zero to no choices.

Case Study #3

Satan's Principal

Mrs. Enu was marking homework books in her classroom. She had five minutes left before her students returned from gym class when the principal, Ms. Arind stormed into the classroom and said, "I need to speak with you! Did you hear the announcement? She repeated this three times while Mrs. Enu tried to respond. "When a teacher coach schedules a professional development with you, I expect you to be there on time. I want to know why you . . . Mrs. Enu interrupted by stating, "You do not know the entire story and if you can stop yelling long enough, I will explain to you what had happened. And, I do not appreciate your accusations and the way that you are speaking to me as if I were a child."

The "teacher mentor" that she was referring to wrote Mrs. Enu a letter informing her about a meeting during her preparation period. Mrs. Enu wrote back to her at the bottom of the letter stating that she would be happy to meet with her; however, she would like a prep payback promise in writing. During the previous week the mentor made a similar request about a meeting but she also stated that she would meet in Mrs. Enu's classroom. Therefore, since the letter did not state otherwise, Mrs. Enu assumed that the meeting would be held in her classroom.

Arind went on to say, "The next time you are ordered to carry materials back you better...." Mrs. Enu interrupted her by saying, "You do not have the right to order me to carry a stack of heavy books or anything else for that matter!" She said, "You know, I WILL WRITE YOU UP FOR INSUBORDINATION!" Mrs. Enu replied, "Go right ahead. In this way, at the hearing, I will get an opportunity to let them know my half of the story and how disrespectful you are to me." As Mrs. Enu was speaking, Ms. Arind waved her hand in her face and proceeded towards the exit. Mrs. Enu was trying to tell her about a recent surgery she had had and it had been agitated by carrying books and other items in her classroom. At this time Ms. Arind was already out the door and totally ignored what she was saying.

Mrs. Enu was a new teacher to the school but had several years of teaching experience. Mrs. Arind was extremely hostile towards her even when she first entered the building during the first week of school. When she glanced over she said to the person that she had been talking to, "Who is that?" Mrs. Enu attempted to go over to introduce her but Mrs. Arind turned away. Mrs. Enu went into the office and the secretary told her that she would have a seventh grade class. She was in complete shock because during the end of the previous school year, Mrs. Enu in a good faith effort called Mrs.

Arind to introduce herself and received the "cold shoulder". Mrs. Enu asked her did she have any plans to attend the workshop over the summer and Mrs. Enu told her that she was planning to attend an educational seminar out of state but she would make every attempt to attend the workshop. Mrs. Arind replied, "When I suggest that my teachers attend a professional development, I expect them to go! I DO NOT WANT MY TEACHERS COMING IN SEPTEMBER BEHIND THE EIGHT BALL!

The eight ball. Wow, at this time Mrs. Enu was wondering who really was behind the eight ball. She gathered herself and attempted to reverse the conversation back to what she had initially called about and that was the grade assignment. She asked her what grade would she have in September and Mrs. Arind told her that it would be a first her second grade. Mrs. Arind was happy because she wanted a lower grade and she could use a lot of the materials she had already made for the first grade students she had in the previous year. She planned to purchase more materials over the summer. But Mrs. Enu found out later that she did not have first our second grade or even third grade for that matter. Although Ms. Arind had nine eight or nine openings in the lower grades, she placed Mrs. Enu in a sixth grade cycle class.

Later on Mrs. Enu learned from the other teachers that there was an African American male teacher in the sixth grade. She took him out and placed him in the second grade. Also a new African American male teacher was assigned to the school. She placed him in the third grade. There were several newly assigned white female teachers. She placed them all in the lower grades. There were one or two new

African American female teachers. She placed two of them in the lower grades and one in the fifth grade. She also placed most of the new white teachers in the new school building and practically all of the black teachers were placed in the old building. The new, brightly lit, gym room was used for the lower grades and the old cramped, poorly lit, gymnasium (It was once used as a storage room) was used for the upper grades. There was little to no equipment in the old gym room except for one rope dangling from the ceiling. The upper grades (fifth and sixth) were not allowed to have Science class because the white science teacher told Mrs. Enu that they were too unruly and she did not want to teach them. Her request was granted.

Observation Day

It was the second week of school when Mrs. Arind came into Mrs. Enu's class to observe. She sat in the back of the room with an ink pen and writing tablet. Mrs. Enu proceeded to conduct her lesson. She acknowledged Mrs. Arind and told her what had been discussed the previous day and what the children were working on that day. There was a student in the back of the classroom with his head down. Mrs. Enu was well aware of this because she instructed the student to lie down before she gave him a note to the nurse's office. He wasn't feeling well. When Mrs. Arind came in to the room and went to the back when sat next to this student and startled him by slapping his arm. He had his head down on the desk. She ordered the student out of the room. Mrs. Enu was disturbed by this. The student stumbled to the door and hung around the doorway. Mrs. Enu told Mrs. Arind why he was there and said that she wanted him to have a note and an escort to the nurse's office because he was not feeling well and she was concerned for his safety. Mrs. Arind gave her a blank look.

During the final cycle period for the day, the phone rang and on the other end of the receiver was Mrs. Arind. "I WANT TO SEE YOU IN MY OFFICE TOMORROW AT 9:30 during your prep time! Mrs. Enu told her okay but she called back and told her that she could speak with her on the same day.

During the meeting, Mrs. Arind said, "THERE'S A FEW THINGS I NEED TO SPEAK TO YOU ABOUT. FIRST OF ALL, I DON'T CARE HOW THINGS WAS DONE AT THE SCHOOL YOU CAME FROM BUT YOU

DON'T HAVE TO SAY MY NAME WHEN I COME IN TO OBSERVE. AND, WHENEVER I SEND A CHILD OUT OF THE ROOM I DO NOT WANT A TEACHER TO STOP THEM. THE CHILDREN MIGHT THINK YOU ARE SHOWING MORE POWER OVER ME AND I DON'T WANT THEM TO SEE THAT!" Mrs. Enu said. "I think that is your perception and not the students. I was concerned about my student and I did not want him to leave the room in that way. He was feeling poorly and I was concerned about his safety". She then looked more bewildered and repeated what she had said. She then told her that learning centers are not necessary and that they are just busy work. Mrs. Enu had her class set up in a learning center format to engage the students in small cooperative groupings. Mrs. Enu went on to say, "I beg to differ with you. Learning centers can be a very substantive part of the learning process depending on how they are used by the classroom teacher. They can be an excellent tool to use as an extension of a lesson or enrichment activity." Mrs. Arind sat in frozen silence.

Mrs. Enu is in a dilemma. She feels that Mrs. Arind is an extremely hostile insecure person and is either threatened by her mere presence or she simply lacks leadership skills. She feels that is both. Mrs. Arind maintains a philosophy of leadership that is archaic and obsolete. The dictatorial "bossy" role is a thing of the past and it is time for her to acquire the "people skills" that is necessary for her to move forward. She could start with being courteous, fair, and respectful to all of the adults in the school. Professionalism is not a word to be taken lightly. It is something that not everyone understands fully. It is a way of life, no matter how temporary but it is only worthy of those that are deserving of it.

Case Study #4

One day a sixth grade class was going to the computer room. They were lined up in the hallway waiting very quietly with their teacher. The computer teacher had a habit of being late to pick them up. She never said good-morning to the students. She told the teacher, "Oh, the clock was wrong downstairs". This had been the third time that she was late and it was always the same reason. After the teacher left, she saw the computer teacher ordering the students to walk down the hallway. This went on for about half an hour. The period was only 45 minutes. She told the students that they weren't ready to come into the room because they were too noisy. When the children finally were released from the prison warden, they were not only tired from walking back and forth and back and forth but they were humiliated and annoyed. This made it difficult for the teacher to get anything done because she needed to address their immediate concerns which took practically the whole period.

www.ingramcontent.com/pod-product-compliance
Lightning Source LLC
Chambersburg PA
CBHW032136090426
42743CB00007B/618